QUEEN ANNE

A PHOTOGRAPHIC JOURNEY

Queen Anne in Southampton. (Courtesy of Andrew Sassoli-Walker, www.solentphotographer.com)

QUEEN ANNE

A PHOTOGRAPHIC JOURNEY

CHRIS FRAME AND RACHELLE CROSS

FOREWORD BY KATIE MCALISTER, PRESIDENT OF CUNARD

MASTER'S PERSPECTIVE FROM INGER THORHAUGE, *QUEEN ANNE*'S CAPTAIN

The History Press

For Zac and Callum

First published 2025

The History Press
97 St George's Place, Cheltenham,
Gloucestershire, GL50 3QB
www.thehistorypress.co.uk

British Library Cataloguing in Publication Data.
A catalogue record for this book is available from the British Library.

ISBN 978 1 80399 641 7

Typesetting and origination by The History Press
Printed and bound in Turkey by Imak

MIX
Paper from responsible sources
FSC® C111584

Trees for Life

CONTENTS

FOREWORD

BY KATIE MCALISTER, PRESIDENT OF CUNARD

Queen Anne made a lasting impression on me the first time I saw her.

As the 249th ship to sail for Cunard, *Queen Anne* is a testament to the rich history that only a company with our pedigree and one which has been in business for 184 years can accomplish.

At Cunard, here in the UK and around the globe we are famous for our beautiful, iconic *Queens* and *Queen Anne*'s introduction into the fleet marks the arrival of a new icon, as she completes a perfect quartet alongside *Queen Mary 2*, *Queen Elizabeth* and *Queen Victoria*.

Queen Anne is our 249th ship in our 184-year history and we are really known around the world for our distinctive and timeless British heritage luxury experience.

With *Queen Anne* we have sought to preserve that, so that she absolutely feels like a Cunard *Queen*, but also to add a thoroughly modern twist, which signifies a new era in luxury ocean travel.

Over the past four years, we have worked with world-leading designers, alongside master ship builders in Italy, to design innovative concepts, founded in Cunard heritage, which will provide the very best in style, comfort, wellness, entertainment and dining.

Queen Anne: A Photographic Journey brings our new ship to life through stunning photographs and captivating stories. This book allows both past and future guests an opportunity to explore the elegance and grandeur of *Queen Anne*. I can't think of a more fitting tribute to our newest *Queen* than this beautiful book.

Katie McAlister

President of Cunard | June 2024

Katie McAlister. (Courtesy of Cunard Line)

ACKNOWLEDGEMENTS

We would like to thank everyone who supported us in creating *Queen Anne: A Photographic Journey*.

Special thanks to: Katie McAlister, President of Cunard, for the insightful foreword and Captain Inger Thorhauge for giving us a glimpse into the perspective of taking command of *Queen Anne*.

Thanks to the wonderful photographic contributors who aided us with this book, including Andrew Sassoli-Walker – who continually supports our writing endeavours with wonderful imagery – as well as Alison Morton, Colin Hargreaves, Luke Morrison, Perry Poussard, Henry Farnam and Rob Henderson.

Thanks to the team at Cunard for their support in accessing *Queen Anne*, with a special shout out to Francis Fred, Lee Powell, Sam Cole, Sam Balls, Celene Pretorius and David Webster.

Our thanks to Amy Rigg from The History Press for supporting us in this, the seventh instalment of our Photographic Journey series, and our eighteenth book. Amy has worked with us since the beginning, and we are very grateful for her ongoing support. Our thanks also to Emma Kennedy, Chrissy McMorris, Ian Pearson, Katie Beard and the rest of The History Press team.

And finally, thanks to our families, friends and the cruising community for encouraging and supporting us.

INTRODUCTION

The 249th ship to wear the Cunard colours, *Queen Anne* is the newest custodian of a brand that dates back to 1840.

While her interiors are distinctly modern, the ship reflects Cunard's storied past in both direct and indirect ways.

The ship has been painted in the iconic Cunard colours, with a Cunard Federal Grey (which is almost black) hull and white superstructure. The ship's funnel is resplendent in the Cunard red with twin black bands. This branding dates to the very first Cunard steamers, though the shape of the funnel has changed over the years.

Queen Anne's interiors are contemporary in design, with an array of eateries, activities and amenities never before seen on a Cunard ship, but some tradition remains. And if you look, you can't help but notice the inspiration *Queen Anne*'s design has taken from past ships. From the curved staircases and glass-clad open wells, reminiscent of *QE2*, to the Golden Lion pub and Chart Room Bar, Britannia Restaurant, and Queens and Princess Grills, the ship shares many spaces with the three *Queen*s that she joins.

As you embark on this photographic journey on board *Queen Anne*, you will undoubtedly notice the blend of modernity and tradition that make this ship stand out from her fleet mates.

Queen Anne in Southampton. (Courtesy of Andrew Sassoli-Walker, www.solentphotographer.com)

Queen Anne's maiden arrival in Southampton. (Courtesy of Andrew Sassoli-Walker, www.solentphotographer.com)

LOOKING BACK

Built by Fincantieri, *Queen Anne* is the third Cunard Queen constructed in Italy. Her handover in April 2024 puts the Italian shipbuilder on par with Scotland's John Brown Shipyard in the number of Cunard Queens built.

The first Cunard liner to be named after a queen was *Berengaria*. Entering service in 1913, the ship was originally called *Imperator* and sailed for the German Hamburg-Amerika line. Created to be a fierce rival to Cunard's own *Aquitania*, *Imperator* joined the Cunard fleet after the First World War. She was ultimately renamed *Berengaria*, for Queen Berengaria, Queen Consort of King Richard I.

But it was not until the 1930s that there was a Cunard liner to bear the title of queen in its name. RMS *Queen Mary* was named by HM Queen Mary in 1934. It was the first Cunard liner to be christened by and named for a living queen consort, and RMS *Queen Mary* captured the hearts and minds of the travelling public.

RMS *Queen Mary* was paired with RMS *Queen Elizabeth* in the 1940s, the newer ship being named by HM Queen Elizabeth, Queen Consort of King George VI. Together the two ships (which served during the Second World War) established the first ever two-ship weekly transatlantic express service. Their place in history was forever secured.

Many thought that nothing would surpass those original Queens in prestige and fame. Yet in 1967, HM Queen Elizabeth II christened the new *Queen Elizabeth 2*. Modern, sleek and fast, *QE2* went on to serve for thirty-nine and a half years, for most of those years as the most famous ship in the world. She sailed a staggering 5.8 million miles – further than any other passenger ship ever.

RMS *Queen Mary* in Southampton. (Courtesy of Colin Hargreaves)

***QE2* in Sydney Harbour during her final visit in 2008.**

If *QE2*'s fame on the high seas was to be challenged, only a Cunard Queen could do it. And so it was, with the 2004 christening of RMS *Queen Mary 2*. Named after RMS *Queen Mary*, the ceremony was presided over by HM Queen Elizabeth II. When *QE2* retired in 2008, *QM2* took up the baton as the last transatlantic liner, and remains the world's most famous active passenger ship to this day.

QM2 was joined by two cruising sister ships – *Queen Victoria* and *Queen Elizabeth*. Christened in 2007 by HM Queen Camilla (then Duchess of Cornwall) and 2010 by HM Queen Elizabeth II respectively, these two ships allowed Cunard to develop as a twenty-first-century brand, offering a modern and comfortable fleet.

QM2 in Adelaide. (Courtesy of Luke Morrison)

Which brings us to *Queen Anne*. The eighth Cunard Queen, she has quite a legacy to continue. Named for Britain's Queen Anne of the eighteenth century, the ship's introduction in 2024 makes her the first new Cunarder in fourteen years.

The ship is certainly breaking the mould, with a highly unconventional naming ceremony taking place on 3 June, a month after the maiden voyage. At the ceremony in Liverpool, the ship's 'godparent' was revealed as the City of Liverpool. This is in addition to the ship's *madrina*, Roberta Mundula, who christened the ship at the float out.

As *Queen Anne* settles into service, it is the hope of many that the ship will prove a worthy successor to the Cunard story.

WELCOME ABOARD

Entering the Grand Lobby of *Queen Anne*, it is hard to miss the central art piece. Spanning three decks, the lenticular artwork designed by Ian Kirkpatrick is the focal point of this room.

The 391m^2 artwork, manufactured by Trade Etching, is made up of three different vignettes which have been etched on to ninety-seven brass panels that stand out from the wall. Thus, as you move around the room, the image appears to change.

The artwork is entitled 'A Cunard Journey'. Viewed from left to right, it depicts a deck scene on a Cunard ship; an image of a stylised ocean liner; and, finally, scenes of Venice, where the ship was constructed.

The lobby acts as a central link, connecting three main entertainment areas. A curved staircase allows passengers to move between Decks 1, 2 and 3, providing access to guest services, bars, cafés and eateries that surround this area.

Comfortable seating can be found on the Deck 1 level, providing a pleasant vantage point for people watching, or a convenient central meeting area in close proximity to the lobby's own café.

ACCOMMODATION ABOARD

A shipboard sanctuary where you start your day, and retire to in the evening, the cabin is one of the most important areas aboard for many passengers.

On board *Queen Anne*, your accommodation grade and price tag vary depending on the luxury, size and amenities offered in each room. All of the rooms have private bathrooms, with some of the highest graded suites offering two.

The different grades of accommodation correspond to the different main dining rooms that guests are assigned to. Ranging from the most basic, though still comfortable, inside Britannia rooms to the highest graded Q1 suites in the Queens Grill category, the cabins aboard *Queen Anne* have been designed for passenger comfort. And, as an extra delight for all guests, a particular effort has been made to ensure cabin bathrooms are of the highest standard yet seen on a Cunard ship.

QUEENS GRILL ACCOMMODATION

The most impressive grade of accommodation aboard *Queen Anne* are the Queens Grill suites. Referred to as the 'Q' category, there are six grades of accommodation here, from the giant Q1 grand suites to well-appointed Q6 suites.

All suites on board offer a high level of comfort and space, with large bathrooms that include bathtubs and separate walk-in showers. A butler is also provided to ensure passengers can have their every (reasonable) whim met.

The top level of accommodation can be found in Q1 and Q2 suites, and with only four Q2s and two Q1s, this is a highly exclusive level of luxury.

DID YOU KNOW?

Chris Frame and Rachelle Cross worked with Cunard to identify the naming theme of the grand suites as well as suggesting the six individual names used on board the ship.

Each of these special suites is named after iconic waterways of significance to Cunard's long heritage, such as: Halifax (Harbour) and Boston (Harbor), named for Cunard's original Canadian and US ports; the Clyde suite, so named because of the numerous Cunarders built on the River Clyde; and the Hudson suite, the river of Cunard's most significant American port, New York.

The two grandest suites are the Mersey and Solent, found on Deck 6. The former is the main waterway of Liverpool, the line's port of origin, while the latter reflects Cunard's current home port of Southampton.

PRINCESS GRILL ACCOMMODATION

Found amidships on Deck 4 to Deck 8, the Princess Grill 'P' suites are the smaller cousin of the 'Q'-grade accommodation.

There are only two tiers of 'P'-grade rooms aboard the ship: P1 and P2, which are both designed in a distinctive red and gold colour scheme. These rooms offer a spacious balcony, decorated wall coverings, a separate seating area, writing desk and ample storage.

Large walk-in showers are found in the sizable bathrooms, while two large televisions offer access to the ship's interactive television system. Additionally, device charging is a breeze with ample power points, as well as USB-A and USB-C chargers both beside the bed and in the sitting area.

DID YOU KNOW?

QM2 had an interactive television system when first introduced in 2004. Utilising CRT monitors, it came with a keyboard and remote control and could be used to order room service and book shore tours. It was removed after only a few years of service.

BRITANNIA CLUB ACCOMMODATION

DID YOU KNOW?

The first Cunard Queen to feature Britannia Club accommodation was *QM2*.

On board *Queen Anne* there are two categories of Britannia Club rooms. Situated forward and amidships, these cabins all feature a balcony and are very comfortable. The décor in the Britannia Club rooms is very similar to the Britannia accommodation, with the main difference being that those staying in the Britannia Club rooms have access to the restaurant of the same name.

BRITANNIA ACCOMMODATION

The most plentiful accommodation aboard *Queen Anne* is the Britannia grade. There are eighteen room configuration options here, spanning from balcony rooms to inside cabins.

Regardless of your choice, each Britannia room is completed to a high standard with deep-blue carpeting accented by Cunard's distinctive gold. Blue-clad walls are complemented by wood-veneer dressers and side tables. The room also features stylised fixtures, such as a circular mirror and adjustable lamp.

All Britannia cabins come with a well-appointed bathroom with vanity, large mirror, toilet and a large walk-in shower that features a glass shower door and height-adjustable showerhead.

RESTAURANTS

While your cabin might be the place you start and finish each day, the restaurants aboard are likely what you will be talking about long after your holiday ends. In addition to the four main dining rooms aboard *Queen Anne*, passengers can also choose to eat at any of the other casual dining and extra-tariff restaurants aboard.

With a steakhouse, wellness café, casual on-deck grill and three specialty restaurants, as well as a gelateria, guests should have no trouble finding something to eat. The only difficulty might be in deciding what to try first!

RESTAURANTS PROFILE

Restaurant	Location	Seating
Queens Grill	Deck 10	Open
Princess Grill	Deck 10	Open
Britannia Club Restaurant	Deck 2	Open
Britannia Restaurant	Deck 2 & 3	Double Seating (lower) Open (upper)
Artisans' Foodhall	Deck 9	Open
Wellness Café	Deck 10	Takeaway
Sir Samuel's Steakhouse and Grill	Deck 10	Reservation Required
Aji Wa	Deck 10	Reservation Required
Pavilion Grill	Deck 9	Takeaway
Gelateria	Deck 9	Takeaway
Tramonto	Deck 9	Reservation Required
Aranya	Deck 9	Reservation Required

QUEENS GRILL

The most exclusive restaurant on board *Queen Anne*, the Queens Grill is found on Deck 10 and accessed from the Grills Lounge. Taking its name from the original Queens Grill installed on *QE2* in 1972, this restaurant on board *Queen Anne* is decorated in a teal, grey and white scheme with gold accents.

Located on the port side, the restaurant offers pleasing views thanks to large windows. The central table for eight sits below a gold chandelier and is used to host big groups. Much of the restaurant is set up to cater for more intimate gatherings, with tables for two and four the norm, but there is also one table for six.

PRINCESS GRILL

DID YOU KNOW?

The first Princess Grill restaurant on a Cunard ship could be found on board *QE2*. It was originally named 'The Grill Room'.

Occupying the starboard side amidships on Deck 10, the Princess Grill is one of the highest rated restaurants on board *Queen Anne*. Sharing its name and identity with the Princess Grill restaurants on all current Cunarders, the space is noticeably wider than *Queen Anne*'s Queens Grill. It maintains an air of sophistication thanks to the choice of a muted colour palette and custom designed seating.

The central entry area of the restaurant is dominated by a crystal chandelier, while cleverly placed dividers break up the length of the space, making each area feel more intimate. With an open seating arrangement, this restaurant serves those passengers in 'P'-grade accommodation.

BRITANNIA CLUB RESTAURANT

Designed to serve diners from Club Balcony accommodation, the Britannia Club Restaurant on board *Queen Anne* takes this concept to a new level. Situated amidships on Deck 2, the restaurant is accessible from the port side, forward of the Grand Lobby.

Hugging the lobby, the restaurant is noticeably larger than the Britannia Club found on the other Cunarders, yet it maintains a sense of intimacy thanks to several dividers that create distinctive zones within the venue.

Portside diners will enjoy views from large windows, while those located at the forward end amidships will enjoy glimpses into the Grand Lobby thanks to narrow, floor-to-ceiling windows.

DID YOU KNOW?

A ship's navigation centre is called the Bridge, because the command centre on the first steamers, such as *Britannia*, was located on a literal bridge that spanned the distance between the paddle wheels.

Those dining in the aft of the restaurant are welcomed by a custom-made tapestry, featuring a stylised paddle steamer reminiscent of RMS *Britannia* of 1840. Small chandeliers dot the room, while diners enjoy maximum choice by way of an open seating arrangement.

BRITANNIA RESTAURANT

Spanning two levels at the aft of Deck 2 and Deck 3, the Britannia Restaurant is the largest and most visually stunning dining location aboard *Queen Anne*.

Taking its name from the first purpose-built Cunarder, RMS *Britannia* of 1840, the restaurant is dominated by a central well with two large, stylised columns that reach from floor to ceiling. Surrounding the well are four etched acrylic panels depicting the Anemoi wind gods by artist John Biggs.

The restaurant offers two dining styles, with Cunard's traditional set seating (early and late) where a table is reserved for the cruise, found on the lower level. Alternatively, an open unreserved seating arrangement can be found on the upper level.

DID YOU KNOW?

RMS *Britannia* is remembered as the first Cunarder, but this is not strictly true. Although *Britannia* was the first ship built for Cunard, one month prior to her maiden voyage Cunard acquired and sent the small steamer *Unicorn* across the Atlantic. Her arrival in Halifax and Boston created intense media interest, paving the way for *Britannia*'s July 1840 arrival.

ARTISANS' FOODHALL

Eating is synonymous with cruising and *Queen Anne* is no exception. On *Queen Anne* the casual dining option comes with a twist, with the Artisans' Foodhall replacing the traditional buffet found on board the other Cunard Queens.

Artisans' Foodhall is made up of a series of serving stations that feature distinctive cuisines sourced from various places all over the world, and meals are served over the counter. In the centre of the eatery, a barista station is available to serve coffee – particularly popular at breakfast.

The restaurant seating areas are flanked by full-length windows that offer unparalleled views of the ocean or port locations when the ship is making a cruising call. Waiters are on hand to offer support to anyone who requires assistance carrying their items to a table.

DID YOU KNOW?

There was no buffet restaurant on the original Cunard Queens, RMS *Queen Mary* and RMS *Queen Elizabeth*.

WELLNESS CAFÉ

A new concept for Cunard, *Queen Anne* introduces their first Wellness Café at sea. This café is situated on the upper level of the Pavilion, with a small servery and comfortable deck seating dressed in pastel cushions or deep-blue coverings.

A unique menu is offered here that focuses on plant-based eating and healthy protein options. Diners can order at the counter and take in the view while enjoying their meal, thanks to large windows on the starboard side of the space.

SIR SAMUEL'S STEAKHOUSE AND GRILL

Although Verandah has been the name of Cunard's grill since the days of the original *Queen Mary* and *Queen Elizabeth*, on board *Queen Anne* the grill and steakhouse takes its name from the line's founder, Sir Samuel Cunard.

With a menu and service style reminiscent of Verandah on the rest of the fleet, Sir Samuel's offers a slightly more casual dining ambiance, serving both luncheon and dinner. A range of items is available for a set menu fee, while a variety of dishes attract a further charge that is reflective of more expensive ingredients.

Set meal prices include starters, mains (called entrées on board Cunard) and desserts. Of the latter, a sherry trifle is one of the signature dishes, served in a tall, cut-crystal glass. Sommeliers are on hand to assist in pairing wines with your dining choice, which can include steak or fish dishes.

DID YOU KNOW?

Sir Samuel Cunard was just one of several co-founders of the Cunard Line. Others included shipbuilder Robert Napier, as well as the brothers George and James Burns, and Charles and David McIver.

SIR SAMUELS

AJI WA

In a first for Cunard, Aji Wa brings a sample of Japanese cuisine to *Queen Anne*'s dining experience. With the growing global desire to indulge in Japanese cuisine, as well as Cunard holding a strong appeal amongst Japanese cruisers, this addition to the ship's dining options is proving popular.

The space is decorated in deep hues, with dark walls and soft furnishings sporting tones of green and red. At the forward end of the restaurant, a sushi train is available with bar-style seating. Alternatively, ample chairs and tables allow for a sit-down dining affair, with both window views and booth seating available.

DID YOU KNOW?

Cunard has been popular in Japan for decades, with *QE2* proving so popular amongst Japanese citizens that she was chartered for use as a hotel ship in Japan twice during her service career.

PAVILION GRILL

The Pavilion entertainment space on *Queen Anne* includes several eateries, as well as plenty of seating. With a retractable glass roof covering the space, it is also usable in most weather situations.

The Pavilion Grill is only one of the dining options in this space, serving menu items including burgers, hot dogs and other street-food-style meals. The food is offered takeaway style, with guests ordering at the counter and collecting their food to eat either by the pool or at one of the tables and chairs clustered near the Grill.

The Pavilion Grill is often busy during the day, as passengers take the opportunity to eat without needing to head back inside or even having to leave their spot by the pool.

GELATERIA

What is a holiday without ice cream? The Gelateria is another of the eateries located within the Pavilion entertainment space. Serving a selection of gelato and sorbets, the Gelateria is a popular option on board *Queen Anne*.

Though the ice cream comes for an additional fee, the location of this little takeaway venue is perfect for a sneaky treat. Many travellers will try the unique and interesting combination of flavours while taking in the sun on the nearby loungers or going for a stroll on the open deck one level up.

SHHH … IT'S A SECRET

While the Gelateria offers gelato for a fee, inside the nearby Artisans' Foodhall there are two self-service soft-serve machines that are free to use, day and night!

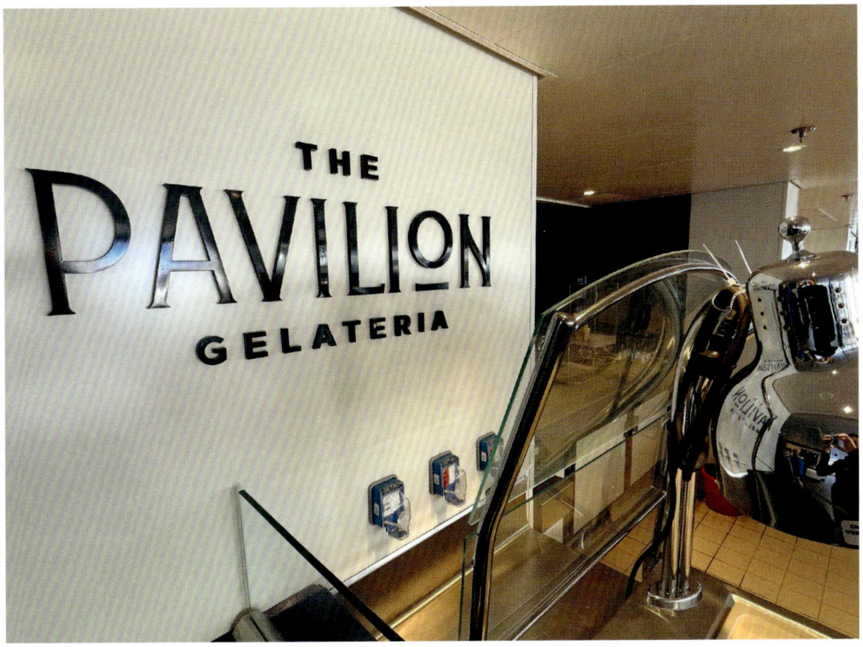

TRAMONTO

Extra-tariff restaurants have become increasing popular with both shipping lines and their passengers over the past few decades, and Cunard has embraced this trend aboard *Queen Anne*, with multiple offerings, including Tramonto on the port side of Deck 9.

Immediately aft of Artisans' Foodhall, this restaurant serves Mediterranean-style food, including Italian, Greek and Moroccan cuisines. The restaurant is delineated from the surrounding spaces by use of different carpeting, window dressings and artwork on the walls. It is a vibrant space owing to the use of bright yellow accents throughout.

ARANYA

Serving a variety of Indian-style foods, Aranya, on the starboard side of Deck 9, is another extra-tariff dining option on board. While the décor is more subdued than Tramonto on the opposite side of the ship, it still manages to impart a sense of space, with the use of themed artworks and decorations.

The restaurant is the first Indian-specific specialty restaurant found on board a Cunard Queen, and forms part of the refreshed on-board offering that *Queen Anne* introduced for the line. Aranya requires a reservation and is serviced by dedicated waiters and its own maître d'hôtel.

DID YOU KNOW?

Cunard were among the first pioneers for the 'extra' special restaurants on board ships. The line introduced the First Class Grill on board *Aquitania*, while the Verandah Grills on *Queen Mary* and *Queen Elizabeth* were legendary for their world-class service.

BARS AND LOUNGES

The vast majority of the organised on-board activities take place within the many bars and lounges on *Queen Anne*. These rooms are also a great place to relax or spend some quiet time reading, getting to know your fellow travellers, or just enjoying a drink.

Located over most of the entertainment decks, the bars and lounges aboard *Queen Anne* each have a distinct atmosphere. Open to all passengers (with the exception of the Grills Lounge and Concierge), these rooms offer a variety of entertainments throughout both the day and night.

BARS AND LOUNGES PROFILE

Bars and Lounges	Location	Best For
Sky Bar	Deck 14	Views over the Pavilion deck
Commodore Club	Deck 12	Forward-facing views
Churchill's	Deck 12	Cigar smoking
Admiral's Lounge	Deck 12	Weddings at sea
Boardroom	Deck 12	Small gatherings
Cabana	Deck 11	Casual drinks with a view aft
Grills Lounge	Deck 10	Pre-dinner drinks for Grills passengers
Pavilion Pool Bar	Deck 9	Drinks to enjoy by the Pavilion pool
Panorama Pool Bar	Deck 9	Grabbing a drink and relaxing on the open deck
Carinthia Lounge	Deck 3	Daytime coffee and tasty pastries
Royal Court Theatre	Deck 2 & 3	Insights lectures and evening shows
Room 1840	Deck 3	Meeting with friends for a drink or gambling at the casino
Queens Room	Deck 2 & 3	Afternoon tea and ballroom dancing
Golden Lion	Deck 2	English-style pub lunches
Bright Lights Society	Deck 2	Interactive shows
Chart Room	Deck 2	Meeting friends, day and night
Games Room	Deck 1	Board and card games
Drawing Room	Deck 1	A quiet area to relax near the Grand Lobby
Grand Lobby Bar	Deck 1	Grabbing a coffee when you're on the go

SKY BAR

For a drink with an unusual view, you'll want to visit the Sky Bar. Located on Deck 14, the Sky Bar overlooks the retractable glass roof that covers the Pavilion entertainment area on Deck 9.

In addition to providing a different perspective on the ship, the Sky Bar also serves the topmost deck space on board, including the pickleball court and putting green. Though the views from the top are spectacular, it can get a bit windy up there, so some patrons may prefer to sit closest to the bar where they are offered some protection from the elements.

COMMODORE CLUB

A signature space on Cunard, first introduced aboard *QM2*, the Commodore Club is located at the forward end of Deck 12 and is the highest indoor bar aboard. With spectacular views out over the front and sides of the ship, the Commodore Club is a very pleasant room to enjoy a drink or spend some time with friends and loved ones.

Its forward-facing view and large windows mean that it is also a popular place to enjoy port entries and exits when the weather is less than pleasant outside.

In addition to being a welcoming place to sit during the day, the Commodore Club hits its stride in the evenings, offering live music and specialising in cocktails and mixed drinks.

CHURCHILL'S

DID YOU KNOW?

In the days of old, passengers had few restrictions on where they could light up. Today things are much more 'fresh air friendly', with only a few areas reserved for smoking.

Smoking is not allowed in most of the inside spaces aboard *Queen Anne*, but Churchill's is one exception: the cigar lounge has been a room on board all of the most recent Queens.

Named for Sir Winston Churchill, who was a noted cigar lover, the Churchill's space aboard *Queen Anne* pays tribute to the Prime Minister who led Britain through the Second World War. With large windows overlooking the starboard side of the ship and comfortable leather chairs, this space is a popular retreat for those who partake in cigar smoking.

ADMIRAL'S LOUNGE AND BOARDROOM

For those looking to get married or renew their wedding vows aboard the ship, the Admiral's Lounge is the venue for the ceremony. Able to be opened up to the next-door Boardroom, the Admiral's Lounge is a bigger space than the equivalent rooms aboard the other Cunard ships.

With a neutral colour scheme and beautiful windows along the starboard side of the ship, the room makes a spectacular backdrop for a special occasion, especially once the room is decorated with floral arrangements courtesy of the on-board florist. There is easy access to the deck outside for photographs, directly through the Boardroom and through the corridor next door.

The Admiral's Lounge and Boardroom are also used for other functions, as separate or joined spaces.

CABANA

DID YOU KNOW?

The Cabana features two horizon telescopes for passenger use.

On the aft end of Deck 11 is the Cabana. Open to all passengers, the Cabana overlooks the Panorama Pool Club, two decks below. The Cabana offers an array of different seating options, including deck chairs, bar stools, tables and cabana lounges.

Wait staff circulate here, taking orders and bringing drinks to passengers whilst they enjoy the outdoors and the fresh sea air. Those who prefer to can order their drinks at the bar.

GRILLS LOUNGE AND CONCIERGE

Passengers who occupy Grills suites are welcome to visit the Grills Lounge, located on Deck 10. The space sits in a central location between the Queens Grill and Princess Grill restaurants.

A petrified tree is the main feature of the Grills Lounge, which sits under a glass roof. The tree is decorated in autumn leaves that complement the teal and mustard colour scheme of the room.

The Grills Lounge serves drinks throughout the day and into the evening. Grills passengers can also partake in afternoon tea in the Grills Lounge.

An exclusive concierge service can be found in this space.

PAVILION POOL BAR

Sitting out by the pool is one of life's great pleasures when cruising in warm climates, but the Pavilion Pool area on *Queen Anne* is also a vibrant entertainment space, hosting gatherings including Cunard World Club parties and dancing.

To satisfy the drinks needs of all these different activities, there is the Pavilion Pool Bar. With plenty of seating around the bar itself and a large service area, it is kept busy throughout the day and night.

PANORAMA POOL BAR

Catering to passengers enjoying the Panorama Pool Club, the Panorama Pool Bar is a popular location throughout the day and during sail-away events. Unlike the Pavilion Pool, the Panorama Pool is open air, meaning that the pool area is not as popular in inclement weather.

The Pool Bar is located under cover, allowing it to still be in use even when it is raining, though many patrons will probably prefer to find somewhere drier to enjoy a drink. When the weather is fine, though, this bar is kept busy keeping swimmers and sunbathers hydrated.

CARINTHIA LOUNGE

Serving light breakfasts and lunches, as well as snacks throughout the day, the Carinthia Lounge on board *Queen Anne* also acts as a coffee shop for barista-style drinks. In addition to serving food and hot beverages, the Carinthia Lounge is also a bar, with alcoholic drinks available for purchase here.

Flanking the starboard side of the Grand Lobby, the lounge overlooks both the lower levels of the lobby and has a view out on to the Promenade Deck. The Carinthia Lounge hosts live musicians as well as gatherings and quizzes.

ROYAL COURT THEATRE

The main show lounge on board the ship, which also doubles as a movie theatre and lecture venue, the Royal Court Theatre offers seating for 825 passengers over two decks.

With a restrained art deco-inspired fit out, the Royal Court Theatre was designed to evoke the music halls of the 1930s. The space offers sloped seating, with particular attention paid to ensuring uninterrupted views from every seat, and is decorated in muted tones.

A large stage features modern, electrically operated equipment to enable full-scale-production shows, while during lectures a branded Insights podium and illuminated light box flank a large screen.

DID YOU KNOW?

The seat rows are labelled with letters (starting with A at the front) that are embroidered on each aisle seat. This gives the space the feel of a shoreside theatre.

CUNARD INSIGHTS

DID YOU KNOW?

Chris Frame presented Cunard Insights lectures on the topic of maritime and Cunard history aboard *Queen Anne*'s maiden voyage.

One of the highlights of the on-board entertainment on Cunard ships is the Cunard Insights programme, where guest lecturers travel on the ship and present lectures about their subject of interest, with topics that range from astronomy, biology and history to sports, true crime and folklore. The guest lecturers travel on both short and long voyages and sometimes only on a segment of a voyage, meaning that the topics and lecturers are always being changed up and guests are offered a wide variety of choices.

In addition to the lectures, the guest speakers also host a question-and-answer session during the voyage, an event titled 'meet the speaker'. This allows passengers to ask further questions about the topic of choice or find out more about the speakers themselves.

Chris Frame lecturing during *Queen Anne*'s maiden voyage. (Courtesy Perry Poussard)

ROOM 1840

The casino and bar on Deck 3 takes its name from the year that Cunard commenced its transatlantic services. It is accessible from the A stairway, the upper level of the Queens Room and also from the deck below, via a stairwell positioned in the middle of this space.

The casino features the expected gaming tables and slot machines. Like many rooms aboard *Queen Anne*, Room 1840 has a curved aspect reminiscent of the open, circular spaces found on board *QE2* decades before. A semi-circular wall divides the space and provides a somewhat hidden area for an array of poker machines.

In addition to the casino, Room 1840 offers a separate place to sit for those who are not partaking in the gaming options. Panels around the bar are lit both day and night, providing a modern atmosphere that is somewhat at odds with its historic name.

QUEENS ROOM

DID YOU KNOW?

There have been five Cunard Queens Rooms, found on board *QE2*, *QM2*, *Queen Victoria*, *Queen Elizabeth* and now *Queen Anne*.

One of Cunard's signature spaces is the Queens Room, their ballroom at sea. While past Cunarders are renowned for the classic style of their ballrooms, *Queen Anne*'s Queens Room is a modern take on the concept.

The Queens Room is a double-height space with seating on both levels and access between the levels via a spiral staircase located at the forward end of the room. The dance floor is oval, echoing the shape of the room. It features a large screen behind the bandstand, which provides one of the focal points for this space.

There is live music played here each evening, and on themed nights the room is transformed with decorations. In addition to dancing, the Queens Room hosts afternoon tea, fitness classes and, on occasion, shipboard parties.

GOLDEN LION

On the port side of Deck 2 is the Golden Lion. A Cunard staple for the last three decades, the first Golden Lion was added to *QE2* in 1994. Sporting traditional British-style pub décor, the Golden Lion serves both food and beverages throughout the day and into the night. While some of the food items are included with the price of your voyage, others incur a fee. Diners will also find an extensive beverage menu here, with particular focus on pub-style drinks and Cunard's branded beers.

In addition to food and drinks, the Golden Lion also hosts a number of activities for travellers to participate in, including bingo and trivia, as well as hosting live musical performances. The walls are adorned with an eclectic mixture of lion-inspired artworks and maritime memorabilia.

DID YOU KNOW?

The name Golden Lion refers to the Cunard emblem, which features a gold rampant lion holding a globe.

BRIGHT LIGHTS SOCIETY

In 1881 *Servia* was the first Cunard ship to introduce electric lighting. While electric lighting is no longer an exciting novelty for today's passengers, *Queen Anne* pays tribute to *Servia* with the Bright Lights Society, located on the starboard side of Deck 2.

As on *Servia*, the electric lightbulb has been made into a feature, with the ceiling illuminated with many exposed bulbs. There is also comfortable seating, a small dance floor and a stage that is popular in the late evening when the room transforms into the ship's nightclub.

In addition to serving as a bar and dancing venue, Bright Lights Society is also a popular show lounge, with custom-designed interactive shows performed here to a small, prebooked audience.

The venue is also home to the Cunard Insights programme's 'meet the speaker' events - held during the daytime usually on the last sea day of the cruise.

CHART ROOM

The Chart Room bar was first introduced aboard *QE2* during its 1994 refit and has become a popular bar on Cunard ships since, missing only from the current *Queen Elizabeth*.

On *Queen Anne* the Chart Room is made up of a series of three interconnected spaces, consisting of the bar area, the main seating area and the 'snug', a cosy area and the aft-most space which was designed for conversation.

Like the Chart Room on board *Queen Victoria*, the designers made the choice to focus on star charts rather than nautical charts on *Queen Anne*, playing into the history of navigation by the stars. This theme is expressed by the star charts on the walls of the rooms, and by the crystal chandeliers. With the bar jutting into the upper level of the Grand Lobby, the presence of this space is felt throughout the central hub of the ship, drawing passers-by in and creating a vibrant atmosphere.

GAMES ROOM

Card games, board games and puzzles can be found in the Games Room on the port side of Deck 1. The room features games tables set for four, with views out over the ocean.

With seating spilling out into the Grand Lobby, the Games Room is also served by the Grand Lobby Bar, making it an even more enjoyable way to spend a few hours.

DID YOU KNOW?

A special chess set was designed for *Queen Anne*. The pieces are shaped for activities and vistas aboard the ship, such as the rooks shaped like the ship's funnel and a pawn shaped like a dancing couple.

DRAWING ROOM

Elegant and comfortable are two words that come to mind when viewing *Queen Anne*'s Drawing Room. The lounge on the starboard side of Deck 1 was designed to provide a relaxed, but attractive, smaller venue for passengers to enjoy some quiet time, or catch up with friends.

With multiple seating options, several desks for working and a small selection of books, the Drawing Room is a great place to spend a few hours.

GRAND LOBBY BAR

The coffee shop on Deck 1 at the aft of the Grand Lobby makes the Grand Lobby aboard *Queen Anne* a vibrant place to sit during the day. Serving specialty coffees and teas, as well as a selection of cakes and pastries, the Grand Lobby Bar might be small, but it is mighty. This bar serves not only the seating area within the Grand Lobby, but also the Games Room and Drawing Room that open off this area.

DID YOU KNOW?

Prior to *QM2*, Cunard ships did not feature a Grand Lobby. Instead the ships had multiple embarkation lounges, which were positioned throughout the ship to cater for the different passenger classes on board.

PUBLIC ROOMS

Comprising the rooms that are designed for a specific purpose and generally more solitary pursuits, the public rooms aboard *Queen Anne* allow for even more ways to spend your day. With options for quieter activities, such as reading and art appreciation, to the more active at the spa and fitness centre, and even the kids-only Zone, these rooms help to make your cruise more enjoyable.

Public Rooms Profile

Room Name	Location	Popular For
Library	Deck 12	A selection of books and great views of the ocean
The Zone	Deck 12	Entertaining the kids
Boutiques	Deck 3	Duty free shopping and souvenirs
Photography Centre	Deck 3	Viewing and purchasing photos taken by the ship's photographers
Beauty Salon	Deck 2	Hair and beauty therapy services
Voyage Sales Office/ Shore Experiences	Deck 2	Getting information about booking new cruises and Cunard World Club loyalty
The Gallery	Deck 2	Viewing art offered for sale on board
Spa and Fitness Centre	Deck 1	The thermal suite and shipboard gym
Purser's Office	Deck 1	Queries and complaints

LIBRARY

A cosy room with sweeping views over the port side of the ship, the Library is located aft of the Commodore Club on Deck 12. Though not the most extensive library at sea, the Library aboard *Queen Anne* does have a wide selection of books.

It is furnished with comfortable armchairs and ottomans, for those who wish to stay and read indoors. There are also several desks for those wanting to work or write, with a beautiful view of the ocean outside, while a librarian is on hand at selected hours to support browsers in choosing something to read.

THE ZONE AND ZONE OUTDOOR PLAY

Kids-only areas allow younger travellers the chance to make new friends and enjoy games and activities, while at the same time giving parents the opportunity to get some time to themselves. *Queen Anne*'s kids-only area is known as The Zone.

Located on the port side of Deck 12, directly aft of the Library, The Zone caters to travellers between the ages of 2 and 17 in three separate rooms and also has its own Outdoor Play area, which is fenced off from the rest of the deck for safety.

Queen Anne has an additional space – the Baby Zone – which acts as a night nursery, allowing parents to have a few hours to themselves while their little ones sleep under the watchful eye of the Zone staff.

The Zone offers entertainment for kids and teens. (Photos Courtesy Alison Morton)

BOUTIQUES

Queen Anne's boutiques are located in two areas, both on Deck 3. The forward shopping zone is found around the upper level of the Queens Room, with the second area located near the Grand Lobby.

Post-lecture merchandise sales and book signings take place here, near the liquor store, as unlike previous Cunard Queens, *Queen Anne* does not have a dedicated book shop. Some maritime history books are still on sale in the Cunard Collection store – alongside Cunard-branded memorabilia, clothing and the all-important Cunard teddy bears.

In addition, *Queen Anne*'s shops stock duty-free items, including jewellery, clothing and toiletries. The shops are designed to integrate within the overall flow of passenger movements throughout the ship, creating a buzzing atmosphere as people browse this space while en route to other shipboard events.

PHOTOGRAPHY CENTRE

Souvenir and formal-night photographs are a cherished tradition for many, and *Queen Anne* caters to this need with shipboard photographers. The images they take can be viewed at the Photography Centre on Deck 3, which also acts as the walkway between the Carinthia Lounge and the upper level of the Britannia Restaurant.

The Photography Centre on board *Queen Anne* is a largely digital affair, with screens available to view the photos taken. There is a small studio area where photoshoots can take place, while photography staff are on hand at selected hours to provide support.

VOYAGE SALES OFFICE

DID YOU KNOW?

It is not uncommon for loyal Cunard travellers to book their next cruise on embarkation day!

Booking your next cruise while at sea is a must for many repeat travellers. With the Voyage Sales Office frequently offering incentives to book your next cruise through them, there is often a steady flow of passengers passing through this space.

Queen Anne's Voyage Sales Office is located amidships on Deck 2, just aft of the Queens Room. It is a much enhanced and expanded space when compared to the Voyage Sales area on past Cunard ships, offering multiple sales desks, a waiting area and impressive views of the ocean.

Shelves in the waiting area contain Cunard brochures, pictorial travel books and guides to provide worldwide inspiration for passengers. This space is also the hub for the Cunard World Club, with voyage sales experts also acting as World Club representatives, capable of answering any loyalty-related queries.

THE GALLERY

Even if you have no interest in art, it is likely that you will visit The Gallery on Deck 2. This space is reminiscent of the Gallery on board *QM2*, with large windows dispersed between the artworks.

If you are dining on the Deck 2 level of the Britannia dining room, you will pass through this space daily. This is because The Gallery is found within the walkway that leads from the Chart Room to the lower level of the Britannia Restaurant.

In addition to the art on display, which is available to purchase on board, The Gallery also hosts occasional art-appreciation evenings and champagne events.

SPA AND FITNESS CENTRE

Like *QE2* before her, *Queen Anne*'s Spa and Fitness Centre is located lower in the vessel than on the ships that came between them. Positioned at the forward end of Deck 1, the spa treatment rooms are located on the port side of the ship, with the fitness centre and studio located on the starboard side.

The central feature of this space is the thermal suite: a spectacular spa area with twinkle lighting on the ceiling and heated benches around the pool. The thermal area is complemented by experiential showers, a cold room and multiple saunas.

For those who prefer to work up a sweat by exercising, the fitness centre offers a selection of gym equipment, both cardio and weights. Passengers can burn off the calories from last night's dinner with a view of the ocean, and maybe, if they're lucky, catch sight of some ocean wildlife.

The Beauty Salon on Deck 2 offers a variety of different treatments, including haircuts; colouring and styling; makeup consultations; and cosmetic beauty treatments. Whether you're getting ready for a gala night, or just wanting some 'me time', the view from the Beauty Salon is quite different than from any salon on land!

PURSER'S OFFICE

Just aft of the Grand Lobby on the port side is the Purser's Office. The place to go to discuss any billing-related issues, currency exchange or to voice concerns, the Purser's Office is the administrative hub of the ship.

The space appears smaller than that found on older Cunard ships, largely thanks to it being positioned in a semi-contained annex near the Grand Lobby. Large screens display useful information while admin staff will often walk the queue to answer any incidental questions and shorten wait times.

LAUNDRETTES

Laundry is one of the inevitable chores of life, but while it might not be the most fun thing to do on board *Queen Anne*, sometimes it is quite necessary!

There is a guest laundrette on several passenger accommodation decks of *Queen Anne*. Each laundrette features washing machines and dryers, as well as an iron and ironing board.

The iron is often hot property on the first day as guests try to remove the wrinkles caused by travel, and the laundrettes remain a highly visited, though rarely photographed, room throughout most cruises.

GETTING AROUND

Though each person will use them multiple times per day, passengers don't often spend a lot of time thinking about the hallways, stairs and lifts aboard *Queen Anne*. Luckily, the ship's designers did spend a lot of time thinking about them, with an emphasis placed on providing good flow between the various spaces aboard the ship.

Since *Queen Anne* has a higher passenger capacity than any of her current fleet mates, it was important to ensure that the lifts and stairs did not become bottlenecks during times of high traffic flow. As a result, there are staircases between Deck 2 and 3 located

at Room 1840 and the Queens Room, and a staircase in the Grand Lobby that connects Decks 1, 2 and 3. These staircases are in addition to the three main staircases and lift banks, labelled A, B and C.

The carpeting in the hallways is designed to help guide you to the closest lift bank, while also being colour coded to indicate which lift bank you are approaching. Within the lift lobby there is bench seating, in case you do have to wait, and a wall-mounted map to help you figure out how to get to where you want to go.

ON DECK

Spending time out on deck is a cherished part of an ocean cruise for many. On *Queen Anne* the outdoor areas include both traditional and less traditional pursuits. In addition to deck quoits and shuffleboard, *Queen Anne* also has a putting green, archery area and Wellness Studio, used for stretching and yoga classes. The ship boasts two large swimming pools (one under a retractable glass magrodome, making it usable even in cooler weather), five whirlpools and even two infinity pools for Grills guests.

Popular On-Deck Spots

Area Name	Location	Here you will find
Observation Deck	Deck 14	Sweeping and sheltered views over the bow of the ship
Pickleball Court/Paddle Tennis, Putting Green	Deck 14	Light sporting activities
Wellness Studio	Deck 11	Yoga classes and stretching mats
Grills Terrace	Deck 11	Seating and two infinity pools
Pavilion Pool	Deck 9	A sheltered swimming pool, whirlpools, food and drinks
Panorama Pool Club	Deck 9	An open-air swimming pool, whirlpools and bar
Promenade Deck	Deck 3	A wrap-around walking promenade

SPORTS AND OBSERVATION DECKS

The sports and open-air games are located across Decks 10, 11 and 14, and include both traditional and not-so-traditional activities.

There are multiple shuffleboard and deck quoits courts located across these decks, which give plenty of space for passengers wishing to try these more traditional maritime pursuits. Those wishing to try something more adventurous may enjoy the archery range.

On Deck 14 you will find a pickleball court and a golf putting green, as well as a shaded observation area that looks out over the bow of the ship. This is the highest passenger deck on board the ship, so the view is spectacular, though it can be a little windy up there, especially while the ship is underway.

GOLF CLUBS & GOLF BALLS

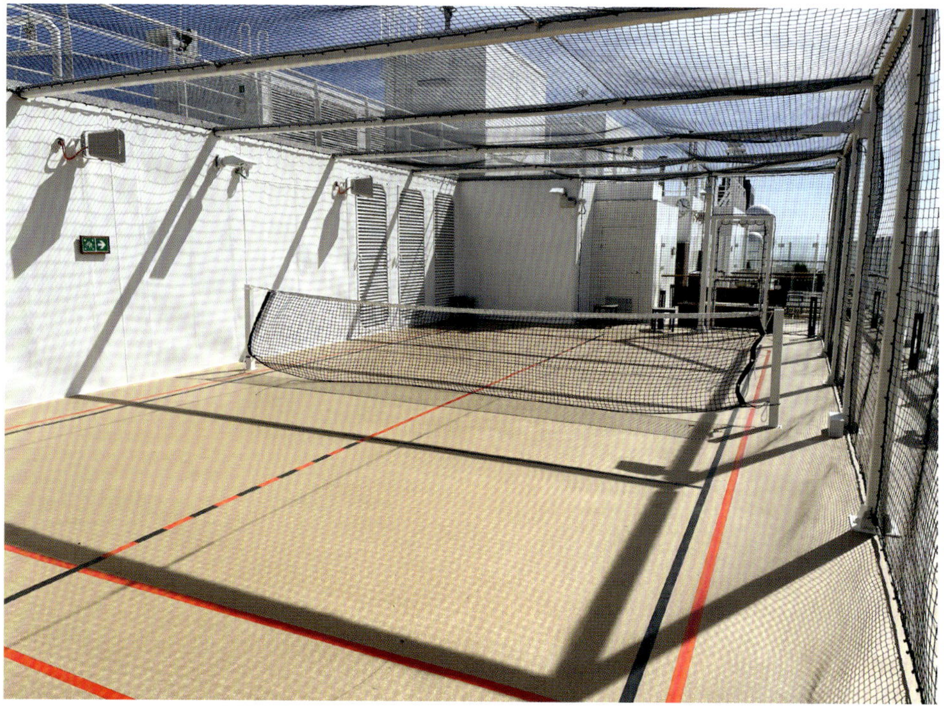

WELLNESS STUDIO

A new addition to Cunard is the Wellness Studio, located on Deck 11, just aft of the Pavilion dome. The Wellness Studio is also covered by a glass roof, which makes the space usable regardless of the weather, and is also sheltered by shade sails.

There is very little in the way of permanent furniture here, with the space used to host activities such as yoga and Zumba classes.

GRILLS TERRACE

The Grills Terrace on Deck 11 is exclusive to passengers travelling Queens and Princess Grill aboard. The Grills Terrace has two infinity hot tubs (one on either side of the ship), as well as plenty of deck chairs and other seating options.

In the middle of the space is the opening for the glass skylight that illuminates the petrified tree in the Grills Lounge below.

DID YOU KNOW?

QM2 was the first Cunard ship to introduce a Grills Terrace, though *Queen Anne*'s is significantly larger, offering more amenities.

THE PAVILION POOL

One of the most spectacular spaces aboard *Queen Anne* is the Pavilion Pool entertainment area. Stretching the whole width of the ship, the pool itself is located in the middle, along with the three whirlpools. This pool is quite shallow, making it popular with families.

The Pavilion Pool is covered by a retractable glass roof, allowing for temperature control as well as protection from rain. The space is triple height, making for a sense of grandeur, and the chequerboard flooring adds a touch of drama.

The Pavilion Pool entertainment space includes a stage and lighting, which allows it to become a late-night party venue and for it to be used for special events, such as the Cunard World Club Party.

DID YOU KNOW?

The glass roof was designed by Martin Francis, who was involved in the construction of the Louvre pyramid in Paris.

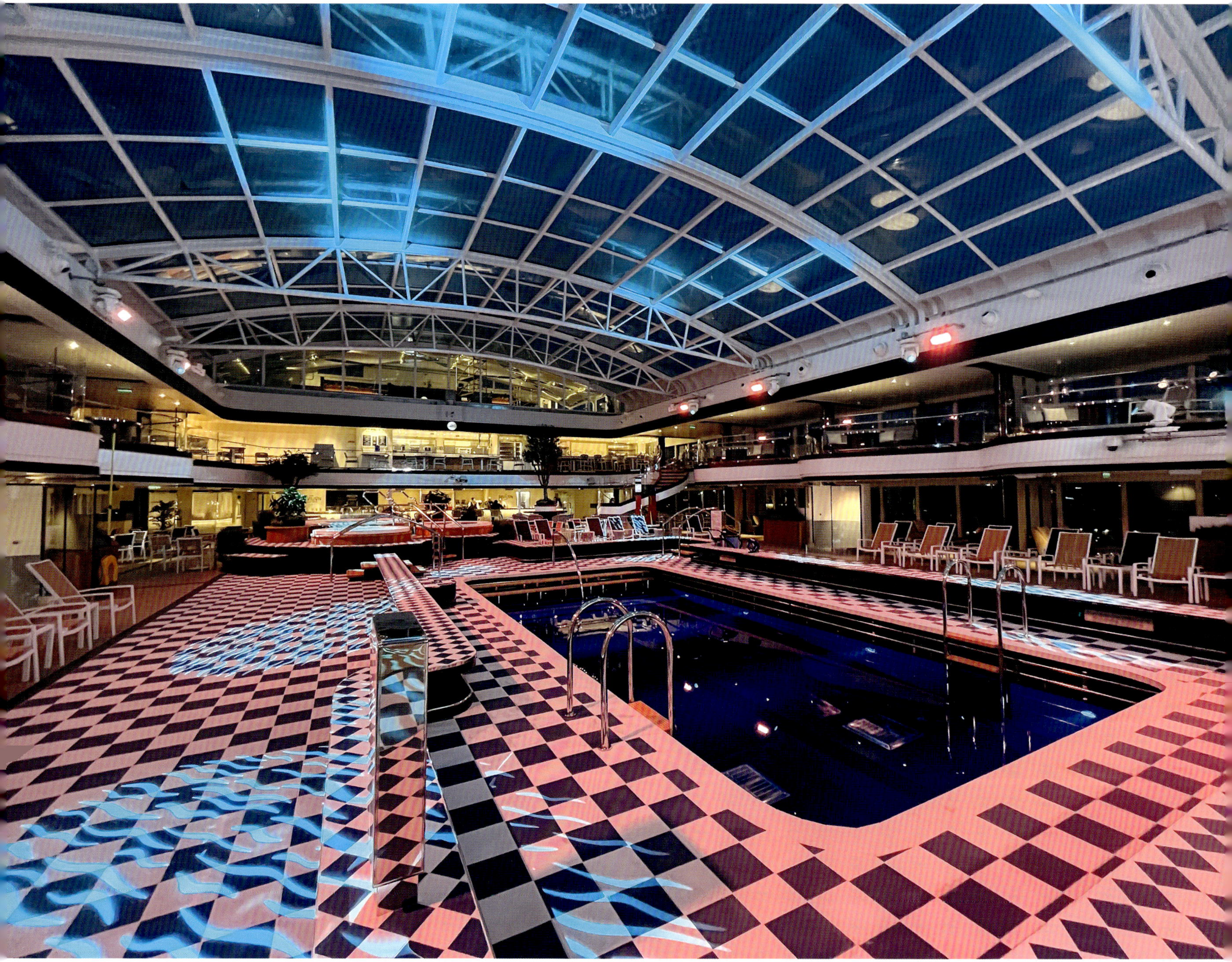

PANORAMA POOL CLUB

On the aft of Deck 9 you will find the Panorama Pool Club. The Panorama Pool is deeper than the Pavilion Pool and is complemented by two whirlpools. There is a stage for live music located at the forward end of the area, while the aft end allows for a view over the stern of the ship.

There are plenty of deck chairs and other seating options located here, with guests able to bring food from Artisans' Foodhall out to enjoy in the fresh air. Staircases on either side of the ship allow access to the open deck above, where even more seating can be found.

PROMENADE DECK

Like all current Cunarders, *Queen Anne* has a wrap-around promenade deck. On board *Queen Anne*, the promenade is found on Deck 3 and offers a number of ocean-viewing vantage points.

A favourite among passengers is the aft observation area, which provides sweeping views over the stern of the ship to the wake below. At the forward end of the deck, sheltered openings give exciting views of the wash created by the bow making contact with oncoming waves.

Unlike previous Cunarders, much of *Queen Anne*'s promenade is sheltered behind the lifeboats, which sit flush against the deck. This provides an improvement in head clearance when compared to *Queen Victoria* or *Queen Elizabeth*, but obstructs the sweeping views usually afforded by this space.

PROFILE

Being a Pinnacle-class ship, *Queen Anne*'s profile shares a common silhouette with several other ships within the Carnival Corporation stable.

The ship's forward superstructure is reminiscent of the Vista-class *Queen Victoria* and *Queen Elizabeth*, though *Queen Anne*'s design incorporates several additional decks above the Bridge, making her far taller.

At 322.5 metres (1,058.1 feet) long, the ship is the second-longest Cunarder ever built, eclipsed only by *QM2*. This makes *Queen Anne* bigger in both length and gross tonnage than the iconic RMS *Queen Elizabeth* – renowned as the largest liner of its day.

The ship shares the same transom stern as her Pinnacle-class contemporaries, adorned with a sizable ducktail. This aids in hydrodynamic efficiency and improves stability. Additionally, the ship features a glass-heavy external profile, with many rows of balconies. This is a design trait that almost all modern cruise ships share as they compete for travellers in the highly lucrative cruise market.

However, there are numerous elements of the ship's design that make her stand out among both the current Cunard fleet and the fleets of other Carnival brands.

QUEEN ANNE
CUNARD

Those with a keen eye will notice *Queen Anne*'s livery is slightly altered from the standard Cunard design, with the Cunard Federal Grey hull paint extending up to just below the top of the hull. This gives the ship an altered forward profile. The vessel's name, situated on the bow, is white against a dark background – another change. So too is the Cunard lettering, which was painted white on black during construction. Ultimately it was repainted red for the ship's maiden voyage.

Queen Anne also carries two Cunard emblems on her hull. These large structures were machined ashore and attached in the shipyard in late October and early November 2023, and feature the Cunard logo.

With *QM2*, *Queen Victoria* and *Queen Elizabeth* all due refurbishments in the coming years, it will be interesting to see if they too receive the revised Cunard livery.

THE MAST

Queen Anne's mast follows a somewhat familiar design to that found on board the current Cunard fleet. Highly stylised when compared to many modern cruise ships, the mast's basic outline is a somewhat more industrial representation of the mast design of *QE2* of the 1960s.

The ship's mast truss is home to two of the ship's radars, located on platforms that jut out from the forward side of the mast. Signal and communicative lighting can also be found here.

Internally, the mast houses a narrow ladder with small doors that allow for access on to the various platforms. Numerous cables and wires are attached to the mast, not just for radio communications, but also to allow the crew to hoist flags such as the ship's flag of registry, the Cunard house flag and the flag of the nation where the ship is calling.

WARTSILA

THE FUNNEL

Queen Anne's funnel incorporates several design characteristics established in the 1960s, while at the same time dropping other well-known elements. Designed by Martin Francis and painted in Cunard's distinctive colours of red and black, the funnel was built on the quayside as a single block and then craned on to the ship in April 2023. It comprises two main elements: the funnel itself (painted black) and the cowling (painted red with black bands). The funnel encloses various pipes and shafts that link the top of the ship with the engine room deep below and ventilates the ship's four Caterpillar-MaK engines, each of which can produce 12,600kW of power.

The funnel also holds two of the ship's whistles, including a 'special' whistle designed to replicate the sound of the original Cunard Queens. Keen observers will notice that, unlike *QE2*, *QM2*, *Queen Victoria* and *Queen Elizabeth*, *Queen Anne*'s funnel does not have the distinctive white 'scoop'. This structure – that directs air up and over the funnel – was omitted from the new ship's design.

BEHIND THE SCENES

While the focus for passengers is on relaxation and enjoyment, for the officers and crew it is a very different matter. *Queen Anne* is a home, workplace and recreation area for 1,225 crew, with extensive areas on board the ship housing a behind-the-scenes city at sea, rarely seen by passengers.

Deep within the ship's hull, engineering spaces are overseen by a team of engineers. Under the direction of the ship's chief engineer, this team of experienced technical experts manage the diesel engines, podded propulsion system, water desalination, plumbing and sewage-treatment systems, and air-conditioning and electrical systems.

While passengers will regularly interact with crew in the bars and lounges, as well as with their cabin attendants, it might surprise you to know there is a sizeable back-of-house team that work around the clock to ensure everything runs smoothly.

Take food, for example. As a passenger, you see your meal nicely presented on your plate – but it takes a lot of work to get it there. Provisions are loaded on board in port,

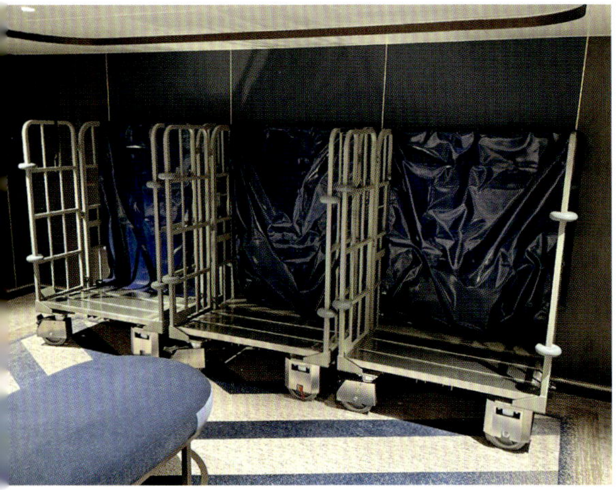

where a team oversee the safe delivery, preparation and storage of the food items for use throughout the voyage. There are massive refrigerated areas under the waterline, where everything from vegetables and fruit to wine and chocolate can be found.

The ship's galleys are also a hive of activity, and it is here that the raw food items are transformed into delicious dishes. Teams of chefs work under the watchful eye of the executive chef, while separate teams oversee the transportation of stores into the galleys and clearance of waste once the meal is completed.

Cruise ships produce a lot of waste, which all must be managed by the crew. There is a recycling centre where items are stored for disposal on land, while food waste is also managed on board and handled in accordance with international regulations.

Another area that travellers see only a glimpse of is luggage management. When the ship is in port, thousands of items of luggage are brought on board. This is managed by a team of porters, with the aid of large trolleys, crew-only lifts and back-of-house alleyways and corridors, to ensure each bag ends up with its owner as quickly as possible.

And finally, one of the most significant jobs on board any ship: maintenance! This is a continual task, requiring a dedicated team who oversee everything from small shipboard repairs to painting, carpet cleaning and polishing the glass magrodome.

Together, the crew bring the ship to life, to ensure that day after day *Queen Anne* will offer the best experience possible to travellers – for years to come!

THE BRIDGE

The command centre of any cruise ship, the Bridge is an essential part of the ship's design and daily operations. On board *Queen Anne*, the Bridge is located on Deck 8, forward. It spans the entire width of the ship and extends past the hull to allow for improved visibility thanks to two fully enclosed Bridge Wings.

The ship's main navigation control is undertaken in the centre consoles, which comprise numerous screens that display the ship's systems in an easily accessible format. This includes electronic chart displays, navigation aids and digital representations of the various shipboard systems, such as engines, fire systems and air-conditioning/HVAC.

Like most ships today, *Queen Anne*'s main wheel is much smaller than expected, though in practice, while in open ocean, the vessel is usually controlled through computerised input or a small joystick around the size of your ring finger.

When in port, or sailing in busy sea lanes, the command team will move to one of the Bridge Wings, which allows for improved visibility along the ship's length. The main navigation consoles are mirrored on each Bridge Wing, along with controls to handle the bow thrusters and azipods.

Queen Anne's whistles are also controlled from the Bridge, with a large central console near the forward windows housing the 'special' whistle – which is designed to sound like the whistles on the original Queens.

BUILDING *QUEEN ANNE*

Queen Anne's entry into service in May 2024 was the culmination of a building period that stretched almost a decade.

With a gross tonnage of 114,188, the ship was announced during 2017, though in reality work had been ongoing behind the scenes to study the design and ensure the feasibility of the Pinnacle-class ship within the Cunard fleet well before that date.

Cunard chose the *QE2* 50th Anniversary Celebration voyage, hosted on board *Queen Elizabeth*, to announce the new ship, which remained unnamed until early 2022. The vessel is the 249th ship to join the Cunard fleet.

The first new ship for Cunard since 2010, *Queen Anne* was designed to appeal to a younger market. As such, the interior of the ship was crafted to be different from the existing fleet.

DID YOU KNOW?

In October 2023, Cunard hosted a group of journalists on board *Queen Anne* at the shipyard. Those in attendance were given tours of the ship led by brand manager Francis Fred and Chris Frame. The tours showcased the interior spaces of the vessel while they were still under construction!

To achieve this, in 2019 Cunard assembled a design team for the public rooms and interior spaces. The team was led by Adam D. Tihany and included designers Simon Rawlings, Terry McGillicuddy, Fiona Thompson and Sybille de Margerie.

Queen Anne was built at Fincantieri, with construction officially commencing in 2019, when the first steel cutting took place. The yard used the unconventional approach of having large parts of the bow and stern built at different locations. Fincantieri's Castellammare di Stabia yard built the bow and lower forward decks, which were launched down a conventional slipway in May 2022. This block was then transferred to Fincantieri Marghera, near Venice, to be attached to the amidships and stern section during a keel-laying ceremony.

Works were significantly disrupted by the COVID-19 pandemic. As a result, the ship's completion date was pushed back during the pandemic to January 2024. This date was later revised to May 2024 to allow the yard sufficient time to complete the ship.

Unlike ships of old that were built on a slipway, *Queen Anne* was predominantly built by assembling several prefabricated blocks while in a drydock. This method of construction allows for large parts of the ship to be manufactured away from the drydock where the ship is being assembled, greatly increasing the speed and efficiency of the construction.

In February 2024 the ship completed her sea trials. This important step allowed both Fincantieri and Cunard to test the vessel, ensuring that speed, manoeuvrability and operational requirements were met. With these essential checks completed, the ship returned to the yard for final preparations for her delivery to Cunard.

Queen Anne's Bridge under construction in October 2023. Wiring and cabling is being installed to link the monitoring systems with the rest of the ship.

Queen Anne was officially handed over to Cunard on 19 April 2024. She left the shipyard on 24 April and entered service on 3 May, with her naming ceremony taking place in Liverpool on 3 June 2024.

DID YOU KNOW?

The bow section of a ship is known in Italy as the troncone.

Left: The Pavilion glass roof is in place, while the Pavilion whirlpools (painted red) are being installed.

Below: The thermal pool on Deck 1 prior to completion.

MASTER'S PERSPECTIVE

When I first joined Cunard in 1997, I never imagined that one day I would take command of *Queen Anne* as her first captain. Back then, Cunard had only one Queen: *QE2*. Her fleet mates were smaller cruise ships, each with their own charm, along with the small ocean liner *Vistafjord* – a ship I remember fondly as my first Cunarder.

Since then, much has changed, and Cunard has grown with a fleet of modern Queens. I was honoured to become Cunard's first female captain in 2010, taking command of *Queen Victoria* and, later, her sister ship *Queen Elizabeth*.

Captain Inger Thorhauge with *Queen Anne* at the shipyard. (Courtesy of Cunard Line)

I was delighted when Cunard appointed me as the master-designate of *Queen Anne*. It's rare for a captain to oversee their ship's construction. It gave me a sense of what it must have been like in 1840 when Cunard's founding captains prepared to take command of the line's first ships: *Britannia, Acadia, Caledonia* and *Columbia*.

If those first Cunard captains from 1840 could see *Queen Anne*'s Bridge, they would be speechless! It is spacious and well appointed, with state-of-the-art technology that aids in navigation.

If the first Cunard passengers could see our public spaces, they would be equally amazed. I too was taken aback when I saw *Queen Anne* transform from a construction site into the beautiful Cunard Queen she is today.

I am particularly impressed with the Pavilion, with its beautiful retractable glass roof designed by Martin Francis. Equally impressive are the new restaurants on board. The selection is sure to impress our modern-day guests. Just imagine what passengers from 1840 would think if they could dine at Aji Wa or experience Bright Lights Society!

Queen Anne: A Photographic Journey offers past guests a chance to step back on board our beautiful new ship, and future guests a glimpse of life on board. Once you have read this book, I have no doubt you will want to travel with us, and I look forward to welcoming you on board *Queen Anne* soon.

Captain Inger Thorhauge
Master, *Queen Anne* | June 2024

QUEEN ANNE FACTS

Name: *Queen Anne*

Namesake: Queen Anne of Great Britain and Ireland

Cruise Line: Cunard Line

Ordered: September 2017

Delivered: April 2024

Maiden Voyage: 3–10 May 2024

Builder: Fincantieri Shipyard, Italy

Cost: US$600 million

Yard number: 6274

Identification IMO number: 9839399

Design and Engineering

Class: Pinnacle-class Cruise Ship

Gross Tonnage: 114,188gt

Length: 322.51m (1,058.1ft)

Width: 35.60m (116.8ft)

Engines: 4 x Caterpillar-MaK 12V43C

Power: 12,600kW per unit

Propulsion: 2 x ABB azipods

Passenger Capacity: 2,996 passengers

GLOSSARY OF NAUTICAL TERMS

Abeam: Off the side of the ship at a 90-degree angle to its length.

Aft: Near or towards the back of the ship.

Amidships: Near or towards the middle of the ship.

Azipod: A propeller pod that can be rotated 360 degrees that acts as both propeller and rudder on a ship.

Bow: The forwardmost part of the ship.

Bow Thrusters: Tubes containing a propeller, which run through the width of the ship at the bow. They greatly aid in manoeuvrability when the ship is arriving or departing port.

Bridge: The navigational control and command centre of the ship. It is so named because the first steamship's command centre was located on a literal bridge that spanned the distance between two paddle wheels.

Cruise Ship: A passenger ship designed to undertake pleasure voyages.

Draft: The depth of water measured from the surface of the water to the bottom of the ship's keel. The draft is important to know in order to safely navigate in shallow waters.

Forward: Towards or near the front of the ship.

Hove To: When the ship is stopped at open sea and not moving.

Hull: The 'body' of the vessel, which stretches from the keel to the superstructure. On board *Queen Anne* this is the part of the ship painted Cunard Federal Grey.

Keel: The lowest part of the ship that supports the constructional framework of the rest of the vessel.

Knot/Knots: One nautical mile per hour. One knot is equal to 1.852km or 1.150 statute miles.

Leeward: The direction away from the wind.

Ocean Liner: A ship designed to undertake passenger-line voyages from point A to point B over an expanse of ocean.

Pitch: The alternative rise and fall of the ship which is often evident at sea.

Port: The nautical term for the left-hand side of the ship when facing forwards.

Quartermaster: On a cruise ship, this term refers to the ship's helmsman.

Ship's Colours: The national flag and/or company emblem flown by the ship.

Starboard: The nautical term for the right-hand side of the ship when facing forwards.

Stern: The rearmost part of the ship.

Superstructure: The body of the ship above the main deck of the hull. On board *Queen Anne* this part is predominantly white and houses the ship's accommodation, balconies and many amenities.

Tender: A vessel or vessels carried on board to provide transport between the ship and the shore. On board *Queen Anne* there are twenty-two lifeboats, six of which are designed as enclosed tender boats.

Wake: A trail of disturbed water left behind the ship when it is moving forwards.

Windward: Facing in the direction that the wind is blowing.

Quick Release
6 metres

BIBLIOGRAPHY

WEBSITES

Chris Frame's Cunard Page: www.chriscunard.com (various access dates)

Chris Frame's Blog: www.chrisframe.com.au (various access dates)

Cunard Website: www.cunard.co.uk (various access dates)

Trade Etching: Leaders in Large Format Chemical Etching For Architecture, www.tradeetching.com/large-format-chemical-etching-for-architecture (accessed 15 June 2024)

PERSONAL CONVERSATIONS

Captain Inger Thorhauge, *Queen Anne*'s Master

Katie McAlister, Cunard President

Francis Fred, Cunard Brand Manager

Sam Cole, Cunard PR Director

PRINT

Cunard Line, 2024, *Queen Anne On Board Printed Material*, Queen Anne Print Shop

Frame, C. and Cross, R., 2020, *180 Years of Cunard*, The History Press

CONNECT WITH CHRIS AND RACHELLE

Learn more about ocean liners and cruise ships by following Chris and Rachelle online.

Web: frameandcross.com

History Website: chriscunard.com

YouTube: youtube.com/chrisframeofficial

Queen Anne's maiden arrival in Southampton. (Courtesy of Andrew Sassoli-Walker, www.solentphotographer.com)